My Canada
NOVA SCOTIA

By Sheila Yazdani

TABLE OF CONTENTS

Nova Scotia	3
Glossary	22
Index	24

A Crabtree Seedlings Book

Crabtree Publishing
crabtreebooks.com

School-to-Home Support for Caregivers and Teachers

This book helps children grow by letting them practice reading. Here are a few guiding questions to help the reader build his or her comprehension skills. Possible answers appear in red.

Before Reading:
- What do I know about Nova Scotia?
  - *I know that Nova Scotia is a province.*
  - *I know that Nova Scotia has a lot of beaches.*
- What do I want to learn about Nova Scotia?
  - *I want to learn which famous people were born in Nova Scotia.*
  - *I want to learn what the provincial flag looks like.*

During Reading:
- What have I learned so far?
  - *I have learned that Halifax is the capital of Nova Scotia.*
  - *I have learned that there are colorful buildings in Lunenburg.*
- I wonder why…
  - *I wonder why the provincial flower is the mayflower.*
  - *I wonder why Nova Scotia grows so many blueberries.*

After Reading:
- What did I learn about Nova Scotia?
  - *I have learned that you can see beautiful plants at Annapolis Royal Historic Gardens.*
  - *I have learned that the provincial animal is the Nova Scotia duck tolling retriever.*
- Read the book again and look for the glossary words.
  - *I see the word **capital** on page 6, and the word **geopark** on page 21. The other glossary words are found on pages 22 and 23.*

I live in Lunenburg. The buildings here are very colorful!

My town was the home of the sailing ship that is on the Canadian dime!

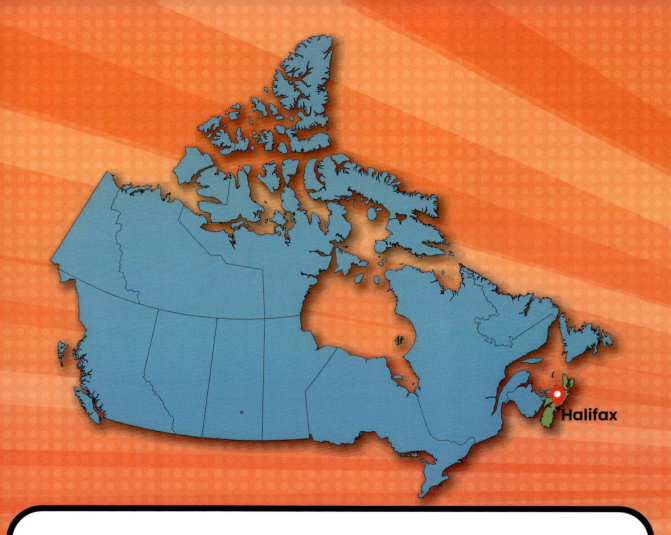

Nova Scotia is a **province** in eastern Canada. The **capital** is Halifax.

Fun Fact: Halifax is the largest city in Nova Scotia.

The provincial animal is the Nova Scotia duck tolling retriever.

Fun Fact: Nova Scotia grows around 22 million kilograms (50 million pounds) of blueberries a year.

My provincial flag has a blue diagonal cross. In the center is a **shield** with a lion on it.

I like to watch the sunset at Peggy's Cove Lighthouse.

Fun Fact: Part of the Cabot Trail, a 298-kilometer (185-mile) highway, goes through Cape Breton Highlands National Park.

My family and I like to learn about history at the Fortress of Louisbourg.

I visit Kejimkujik National Park and learn about how the **Mi'kmaq** lived.

Singer Sarah McLachlan was born in Nova Scotia. NHL hockey player Sidney Crosby was also born in Nova Scotia.

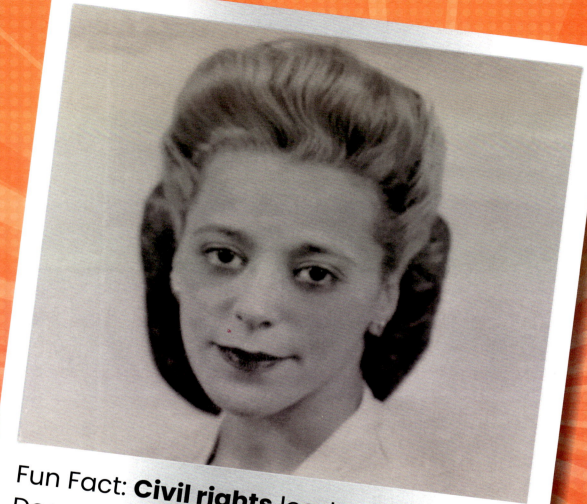

Fun Fact: **Civil rights** leader Viola Desmond was born in Halifax, Nova Scotia.

It's fun to go hiking at the Cliffs of Fundy **Geopark**.

Glossary

capital (CAP-ih-tuhl): The city or town where the government of a country, state, or province is located

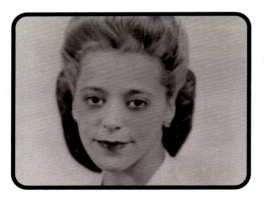

civil rights (SIV-uhl rahyts): The rights every person should have in their country

geopark (JEE-oh-park): A protected area with an important natural landscape

 **Mi'kmaq** (MEEG-em-ahk): First Nations people who are among the first inhabitants of Canada

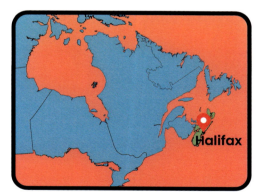 **province** (PROV-ins): One of the large areas that some countries, such as Canada, are divided into

 **shield** (sheeld): A picture that is shaped like a soldier's shield

Index

backpacking 15
blueberries 10, 11
Cliffs of Fundy Geopark 21
Halifax 6, 7, 19
Lunenburg 4, 5
McLachlan, Sarah 18

Written by: Sheila Yazdani
Designed and Illustrated by: Bobbie Houser
Series Development: James Earley
Proofreader: Melissa Boyce
Educational Consultant: Marie Lemke M.Ed.

About the Author

Sheila Yazdani lives in Ontario near Niagara Falls with her dog Daisy. She likes to travel across Canada to learn about its history, people, and landscape. She loves to cook new dishes she learns about. Her favorite treat is Nanaimo bars.

Photographs:
Alamy: Stuart Forster: p. 17, 23; Imago History Collection: p. 19, 22
Newscom: ARCHIE CARPENTER/UPI: p. 18 right
Shutterstock: Geoff Pinkney: cover; Greenseas: p. 3; Brendan Riley: p. 4; Paul McKinnon: p. 5; Media Guru: p. 6, 22-23; Mario Hagen: p. 7; Marina Plevako: p. 8; Jeff Holcombe: p. 9; Bryan Pollard: p. 10-11; Krasula: p. 11; KRS: p. 12, 23; Denna Jiang: p. 13; Natalia Bratslavsky: p. 14; David P. Lewis: p. 14-15; Alessandro Cancian: p. 16; a katz: p. 18 left; Reimar: p. 20; Earl Dow: p. 21-22

Crabtree Publishing

crabtreebooks.com   800-387-7650
Copyright © 2025 Crabtree Publishing
All rights reserved. No part of this publication may be reproduced, stored in a retrieval system or be transmitted in any form or by any means, electronic, mechanical, photocopying, recording, or otherwise, without the prior written permission of Crabtree Publishing. In Canada: We acknowledge the financial support of the Government of Canada through the Canada Book Fund for our publishing activities.

Printed in Canada/012024/CP20231127

Published in Canada
Crabtree Publishing
616 Welland Avenue
St. Catharines, Ontario
L2M 5V6

Published in the United States
Crabtree Publishing
347 Fifth Avenue
Suite 1402-145
New York, New York, 10016

Library and Archives Canada Cataloguing in Publication
Available at Library and Archives Canada

Library of Congress Cataloging-in-Publication Data
Available at the Library of Congress

Hardcover: 978-1-0398-3852-9
Paperback: 978-1-0398-3937-3
Ebook (pdf): 978-1-0398-4018-8
Epub: 978-1-0398-4090-4